Delectable Denmark Recipes

A Complete Cookbook of Delicious Danish Dish Ideas!

BY: Allie Allen

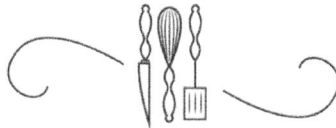

COOK & ENJOY

Copyright Notes

Table of Contents

Introduction

What's the best way for you to create tasty Danish dishes with ingredients that are the same or quite similar to those used in recipes in Denmark?

Thumb through the amazing recipes in this illustrated cookbook.

How do Danish ingredients lend themselves to delicious meals in other parts of the world?

Danish dishes are flavorful and hearty. The Danes use their spices cleverly, in techniques that go back many years. Their expertise in preparing foods, once often served to traditional farming families, is now readily available to people all over the world, so you'll be happy to recreate some of the dishes at home.

Typical Denmark recipes include potatoes or bread to offer starches and carbs, and they are often served alongside dishes with fish, meat and vegetables. The Danes use many fresh and tasty vegetables great. Their dishes focus not only on the taste of the ingredients but also on the aroma and appearance.

In this easy to follow cookbook, you can discover authentic ways to prepare 30 different Danish dishes. From breakfast, lunch and dinner to desserts and appetizers, you'll find all kinds of recipes from Denmark that will tempt you. Turn the page and try out some of the recipes that sound the tastiest to you…

Breakfast Recipes from Denmark...

1 – Danish Bread Porridge

This breakfast dish is not what you probably think of when you hear the word "porridge." It's made with rye bread and beer, and yes, it IS served for breakfast.

Makes 4 Servings

Cooking + Prep Time: 45 minutes + overnight soaking of bread pieces

Ingredients:

- 8 slices of bread, rye - torn
- 1 x 22-fluid oz. bottle of beer, your choice
- 2-3 tbsp. of honey, pure
- 1 handful of raisins, dark or golden
- 1/4 tsp. of salt, sea
- 2 tsp. of cinnamon, ground
- 1 orange, fresh, juice & zest

Instructions:

The night before you prepare this breakfast, tear rye bread in small pieces. Place them in a medium bowl. Pour beer over the top and allow the bread to soak overnight.

The next morning, pour the beer & soaked bread in large-sized pot. Add orange zest, cinnamon, raisins and honey. Bring to boil over med-high, occasionally stirring so porridge won't stick to pot.

Reduce heat. Allow porridge to simmer while regularly stirring, till bread breaks down and porridge is somewhat smooth in texture. Break up large bread pieces, if any.

Remove pot from heat. Add orange juice and mix well. Spoon into individual bowls. Serve promptly.

2 – Denmark Breakfast Pastry

These breakfast pastries are delicious and easily made. Cream cheese and fruit Danish are perfect for a weekday or weekend breakfast.

Makes Various # of Servings

Cooking + Prep Time: 40 minutes

Ingredients:

- 2 sheets of thawed dough, puff pastry
- 1 x 8-oz. block of cream cheese, reduced fat
- 1 tbsp. of sour cream, light
- 3 tbsp. of sugar, granulated
- 2 tsp. of lime juice, bottled or fresh
- Zest of 1 lime, fresh
- 2 & 1/2 tsp. of vanilla extract, pure
- Blueberries, fresh, as desired
- Strawberries, fresh, halved and de-stemmed, as desired
- To brush: 3 tbsp. of unsalted butter, melted
- Sugar, sanding (large crystal), as desired
- Garnish, optional: extra lime zest, fresh

Instructions:

Place oven rack in center slot. Preheat oven to 400F. Line two cookie sheets with baking paper.

Unfold sheets of puff pastry on floured work surface. Using a 4 & 1/2" biscuit or round cookie cutter, slice out four rounds of pastry dough per sheet. Score rounds lightly with smaller biscuit or cookie cutter.

Transfer rounds to lined cookie sheets. Gather dough scraps together. Roll them out and make two to three additional pastry rounds. Add to cookie sheets.

In stand mixer bowl, add sour cream, cream cheese, lime juice, sugar, vanilla and lime zest. Mix till ingredients are combined well and you have a creamy, smooth consistency.

Place 2 tbsp. of this mixture in middle of pastry rounds. Spread out over rounds, leaving 1/4 inch bare at the outsides.

Arrange the blueberries on 1/2 of pastry rounds. Arrange the strawberries on remainder of rounds.

Bake in 400F oven for 13-15 minutes, till edges of pastries are a light golden brown in color. Allow pastries to set on cookie sheets to cool down. Sprinkle extra lime zest on the strawberry pastries, if desired. Serve along with tea, orange juice, milk or coffee.

3 – Eggs & Eel Danish Breakfast

Eels for breakfast? Really? If you've never had this dish, give it a try, and it may well surprise you. The eel flavor blends well with scrambled eggs.

Makes 4-6 Servings

Cooking + Prep Time: 20 minutes

Ingredients:

- 1/3 cup of milk, whole
- 4 eggs, large
- 1 blob butter, unsalted
- 1 eel, smoked
- 6 optional bread slices – you can use baguettes if you like
- For bread: butter, unsalted
- Chives, as desired
- Salt, kosher, as desired
- Pepper, black, as desired

Instructions:

Whisk milk and eggs together. Season as desired.

Melt butter in pan on med. heat and don't allow it to brown at all.

Add egg mixture to pan. Allow it to heat a bit, just till it is slightly firm on bottom, and don't allow egg to brown, either.

Turn egg mixture over. When mass of egg mixture has nearly hardened, remove pan from heat. Allow egg to rest for several minutes, so it can set.

Divide eel into eight to 12 pieces.

Butter six bread slices. Add pieces of eel and eggs on the top.

Use chopped, fresh chives to garnish, as desired. Serve.

4 – Breakfast Buns

If you're a lover of breads and poppy seeds, these breakfast buns are for you. They are not too sweet or buttery, but they're still delicious and soft.

Makes 4 Servings

Cooking + Prep Time: 45 minutes

Ingredients:

- 4 rolls/buns, soft
- 2 tbsp. of melted butter, unsalted
- For the egg wash: 1 beaten egg, large
- Poppy seeds, for topping

Instructions:

Preheat oven to 375F.

Brush buns with beaten egg. Then sprinkle with the poppy seeds. Cut tops with knife.

Place buns on cookie sheet in 375F oven for 25-30 minutes, till buns turn golden in color. Remove from oven and serve.

5 – Danish Pancakes with Bacon & Eggs

"Pancakes" in Denmark are almost like omelets or crepes. They make a wonderful breakfast when served with perennial morning favorites bacon & eggs.

Makes 3 Servings

Cooking + Prep Time: 1/2 hour

Ingredients:

- 5 bacon slices, lean
- 6 eggs, large
- 1 tbsp. of flour, all-purpose
- 1/4 cup of milk, 2%
- 1/4 tsp. of salt, kosher – omit if you're on a low salt diet
- 1/2 tsp. of pepper, ground
- 1 tbsp. of chives, fresh, minced

Instructions:

Fry bacon in non-stick pan. It should be a bit pliable, so don't overcook it.

Combine milk, cracked eggs, flour, salt (if using) & pepper in mixing bowl. Lightly whisk till combined well.

After bacon has cooked, remove it and place on plate lined with paper towels. Allow it to drain. Leave 2 tbsp. of bacon fat or more in pan, for frying eggs.

To same skillet over med. heat, add egg mixture. Cook as you would an omelet, lifting gently around edges to allow runny egg mixture to run under and cook.

Reduce heat level to low. Allow pancake to cook till almost set, 10 to 12 minutes or so. Add bacon. Cook, still over low heat, till pancake has set.

Sprinkle pancake with chives. Serve.

Danish Lunch, Dinner, Side Dish & Appetizer Recipes...

6 – Champagne Roasted Ham

This is tasting champagne like you never have before, and the ham will be so tender, you'll adore it. It's an excellent choice for dinner with guests or for special events.

Makes 6 Servings

Cooking + Prep Time: 3 hours & 55 minutes

Ingredients:

- 15 lb. of ham
- 1/2 tsp. of thyme
- 5 garlic cloves
- 1 cup of sugar, brown
- 12 fluid oz. of champagne
- 1 chopped onion, large
- 2 tbsp. of flour, all-purpose

Instructions:

Preheat the oven to 350F.

Cut garlic in small pieces. Press them inside ham.

Place ham in large roasting pan. Cover fully with filtered water. Bring to boil on med-high heat.

Sprinkle thyme over the ham.

Cover ham. Roast in 350F oven for two hours.

Drain stock from ham, reserving two cups for later.

Remove fat from ham.

Pour two cups reserved stock over ham. Add champagne.

Return pan to oven for 1/2 hour, basting frequently.

Drain stock off and reserve for later.

Sprinkle sugar over ham. Add the onions to pan.

Increase oven temperature to 500F. Roast till ham is brown and glazed. Remove to a warmed, large platter.

In medium bowl, mix the stock with flour.

Cook stock mixture on low heat and stir constantly till you have a smooth texture.

Carve the ham. Serve with stock sauce.

7 – Pork "Frickadeller" Meatballs

This is a great meatball recipe! It uses lemon zest that gives the meatballs a unique and delicate flavor. It's a very tasty recipe that's simple to make.

Makes 4 Servings

Cooking + Prep Time: 35 minutes

Ingredients:

- 2 lb. of lean, finely ground pork
- 1/2 cup of flour, all-purpose
- 1 egg, large
- 1 tbsp. of grated onion
- 1 tsp. of grated lemon rind, fresh
- 1 tsp. of salt, kosher
- 1/2 tsp. of pepper, black
- 1/2 cup of club soda – you can substitute water if you need to
- 4 tbsp. of butter, unsalted
- 2/3 cup of cream, heavy or light

Instructions:

Combine the first seven ingredients and blend well.

Stir in club soda gently. Use your hands to shape meat into 1-2" balls.

Heat the butter on medium heat in non-stick skillet. Add meatballs and brown them on each side. Lower the heat to med-low. Gently cook till done, 18-20 minutes. Transfer meatballs to heated serving dish. Keep them warm.

Add the cream to juices in pan. Bring up to speedy boil while constantly stirring. Pour mixture over meatballs. Serve.

8 – Denmark Beet Soup

The winters in Scandinavia are bitter, wet and very cold. That's why hearty recipes like this beet soup are so popular.

Makes 6 Servings

Cooking + Prep Time: 3 & 1/4 hours

Ingredients:

- 12 beets, large
- 2 lb. of beef short ribs
- 1/2 cup of lemon juice, fresh if available
- 1/2 cup of sugar, white
- 1 chopped onion, large
- 1 tsp. of allspice, ground
- Salt, kosher, as desired
- Pepper, white, as desired
- For garnishing: sour cream, light

Instructions:

Wash beets in cold, clean water. Scrape off their outer skins using a sharpened knife. Cut in small cubes.

Net, place all ingredients except for sour cream in casserole dish. Cover with water.

Cover casserole dish. Then, allow it to simmer on low heat for two hours & 30 minutes. Use a sieve to remove the beef ribs. Garnish with sour cream and serve.

9 – Danish Mansaka

This traditional casserole has been passed down through generations in Denmark. Meat, spices and vegetables combine to make it quite tasty, and it's easy to make, too.

Makes 6 Servings

Cooking + Prep Time: 55 minutes

Ingredients:

- 1 & 1/2 lb. of beef, ground
- 2 cups of onions, sliced
- 1 tbsp. of shortening
- 1 garlic clove, minced
- 1 tbsp. of flour, all-purpose
- 1 & 1/2 tsp. of salt, kosher
- 1/4 tsp. of pepper, ground
- 1 tsp. of sugar, granulated
- 1 tsp. of basil, dried
- 1/2 tsp. of cinnamon, ground
- 1/2 tsp. of oregano, dried
- 1 x 4-oz. can of drained mushrooms
- 1 x 15-oz. can of tomato sauce, no salt added
- 4 thin-sliced potatoes, medium
- 1 cup of Swiss cheese shreds

Instructions:

Melt shortening in large-sized skillet on med-high. Add ground beef. Stir while cooking so the beef crumbles, till it has browned evenly. Add garlic and onions and combine. Cook till they become tender. Drain off excess grease.

Add salt, flour, pepper, basil, sugar, oregano and cinnamon and combine. Stir in tomato sauce and mushrooms. Simmer on low heat for 12-15 minutes.

Place potatoes in glass dish. Cook for 5-6 minutes in the microwave, while occasionally stirring, till they are halfway cooked.

Preheat oven to 350F.

Layer 1/2 of potatoes in bottom of 13" x 9" casserole dish. Spread 1/2 of meat sauce atop potatoes. Sprinkle 1/2 of cheese on top. Repeat layers, with the top layer being cheese.

Bake in 350F oven for 30-35 minutes, till cheese has browned and potatoes have become tender. Serve while hot.

10 – Pork Tenderloin & Vegetables

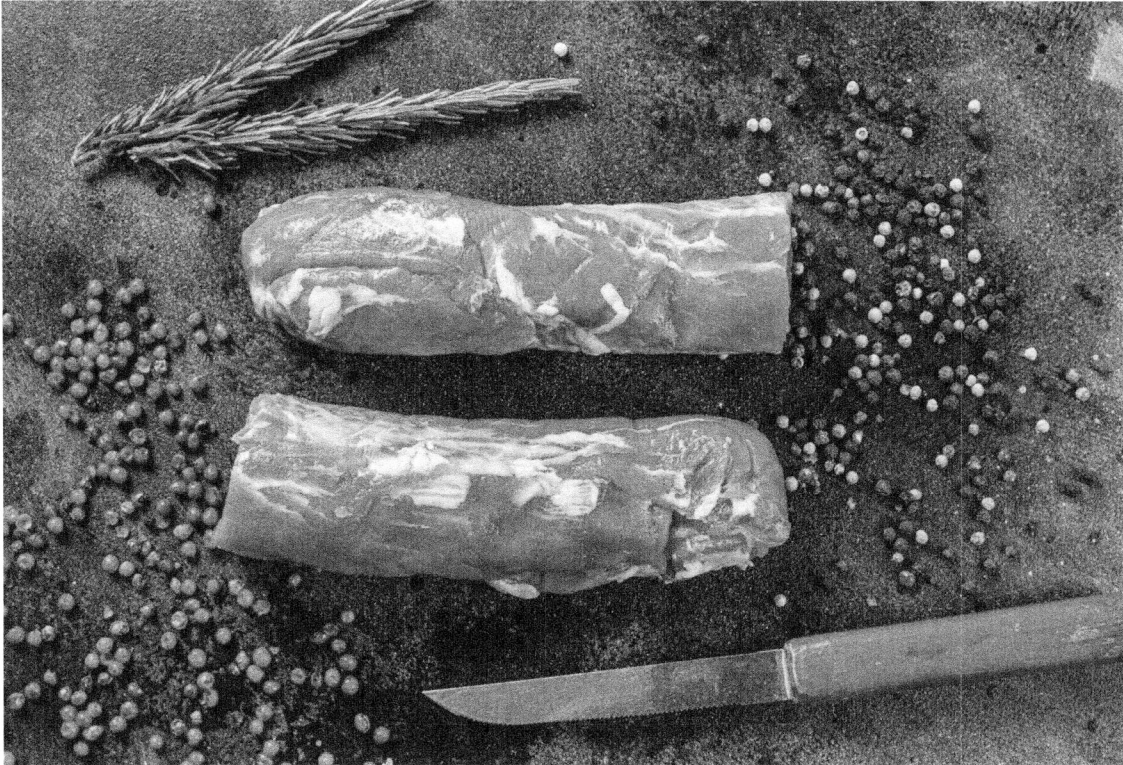

Tenderloin & root vegetables have long been staples in the diet of Denmark. This traditional dish is as hearty as it is delicious.

Makes 4 Servings

Cooking + Prep Time: 1 hour & 35 minutes + 1 hour marinating time

Ingredients:

- 1 pork tenderloin, lean
- 1 lb. of artichokes, fresh
- 2 roots of parsley
- 4 parsnips, fresh
- 2 pears, fresh
- 1 fennel, fresh
- 1/2 bottle of wine, white
- 4 oz. of chicken stock, low sodium

For the marinade:

- 4 garlic cloves, crushed
- 1 fresh lemon, juice and shredded peel
- 4 oz. of oil, olive
- 3 tbsp. of rosemary, freshly chopped
- Salt, kosher, as desired
- Pepper, black, as desired

Instructions:

Preheat oven to 400F.

Trim tendons and fat from tenderloin. Cut in 1"-thick steaks.

Combine garlic marinade ingredients in medium bowl.

Turn steaks in marinade. Place in refrigerator for one hour to marinate.

Clean artichokes. Slice thinly. Peel parsnips and parsley. Cut in cubes.

Wash fennel. Cut in cubes.

Peel the pears. Remove cores and halve pears into boats.

Place pears and veggies in a baking dish. Add wine and chicken stock.

Place steaks atop veggies and pears. Pour remainder of marinade over the top.

Cook in 400F oven for 25 to 30 minutes. Serve from baking dish.

11 – Danish Sigtebrod Rye Bread

This traditional rye bread is easy to make using your bread machine. It's spiced nicely and makes a perfect bread for open-faced Danish sandwiches.

Makes 2 loaves

Cooking + Prep Time: 3 hours & 20 minutes

Ingredients:

- 1 cup of milk, 2%
- 1 cup of water, filtered
- 3 tbsp. of butter, unsalted
- 1/2 cup of molasses, light
- 1/3 cup of sugar, granulated
- 1 tbsp. of orange zest, fresh, grated
- 1 tbsp. each of cardamom, caraway seeds, anise seeds and fennel seeds
- 1 tsp. of salt, kosher
- 2 x 1/4-oz. pkgs. of dry yeast, active
- 1/2 cup of water, warm
- 2 cups of flour, rye
- 5 cups of flour, all-purpose
- 3 tbsp. of melted butter, unsalted

Instructions:

Preheat the oven to 375F.

Next, heat the milk in medium-sized pan till scalding hot. Small bubbles should form around edges. Don't allow milk to boil.

Remove from the heat. Add and stir in filtered water, unsalted butter, light molasses, white sugar, grated orange zest, caraway seeds, anise seeds, cardamom, fennel seeds & kosher salt. Then, allow mixture to cool for 1/2 hour.

Add warmed water to bread maker and stir in yeast. Allow to sit undisturbed for five minutes. Pour cooled milk/spice mixture in with yeast mixture in bread maker. Add flour. Run on dough cycle.

Then, grease 2 x 9" x 5" loaf pans. After dough cycle has completed, remove dough from bread machine. Divide into halves and form them into two loaves. Place in greased loaf pans. Cover. Allow dough to rise for 1/2 hour.

Lastly, bake bread in 375F oven for 35-40 minutes, till you can tap them on bottom and the sound is hollow. Brush still-hot loaves with the melted butter and allow to cool a bit. Serve.

12 – Caramelized Potatoes

These delicious potatoes are often served with family-style meals like roast pork or roast beef. They are also very popular at dinner tables during Christmas & Easter seasons.

Makes 4 Servings

Cooking + Prep Time: 40 minutes

Ingredients:

- 20 oz. of potatoes, small
- 3 tbsp. of butter, unsalted
- 1 cup of sugar, granulated

Instructions:

Boil skin-on potatoes till they have cooked through. Peel off skins and cut in small pieces. Allow them to cool.

Add sugar to medium frying pan. Place butter atop sugar. Heat slowly on med. heat till sugar melts and has started turning brown.

After sugar has caramelized, add potato pieces. Turn them in sugar for 5 to 10 minutes, till the sugar is sticking to them. Serve with meat or poultry.

13 – Danish Torsk Cod Fillets

The popular Torsk dish is made with cod fillets that are broiled & buttered. You'll use frozen fish, and you don't need to defrost it before using it.

Makes 6 Servings

Cooking + Prep Time: 35 minutes

Ingredients:

- 6 x 6-oz. cod fillets
- 6 cups of water, filtered
- 1 cup of sugar, granulated
- 2 tbsp. of salt, kosher
- 1 & 1/2 cups of melted butter, unsalted
- A dash of paprika, sweet

Instructions:

Preheat the broiler. Grease a baking sheet lightly.

Place fish in large pan. Mix water, salt & sugar together in medium bowl and pour over fish. The fish should be covered fully. If it's not, just pour in additional water.

Bring water to boil on med-high and boil for three to five minutes.

Remove fish from the water. Pat with paper towels, removing excess. Brush using 6 tbsp. of melted, unsalted butter. Use paprika to sprinkle.

Broil fish for 8-10 minutes for each 1" thickness, till fillets have turned golden brown in color. Serve along with the rest of the melted butter.

14 – Scalloped Potatoes

The Danish use potatoes a lot in their everyday meals. This recipe is for scalloped potatoes, which pair especially well with roasts or steaks.

Makes Various # of Servings

Cooking + Prep Time: 1 hour & 40 minutes

Ingredients:

- 5 or 6 lb. of potatoes, peeled, sliced
- 1 tsp. of nutmeg, ground
- 4 sliced onions, large
- 1 bundle of rosemary, fresh
- 4 garlic cloves, crushed
- Salt, kosher, as desired
- Pepper, black, as desired
- 30 to 35 fluid oz. of cream, light

Instructions:

Preheat oven to 400F.

Peel potatoes. Slice thinly. Slice onions.

Add potatoes & onions to large baking dish.

Add the cream, rosemary, garlic and lightly stir. Season as desired.

Place baking dish in 400F oven and cook for an hour. Serve while hot.

15 – Danish Chicken Pate

This pate is traditionally served at lunchtime in Denmark. It is often spread on rye bread, then topped with tomatoes or cucumbers.

Makes 12 Servings

Cooking + Prep Time: 1 & 1/4 hours

Ingredients:

- 2 tbsp. of flour, all-purpose
- 1 tsp. of water, filtered, +/- as you need it
- 1 lb. of trimmed chicken livers
- 1 & 1/4 cups of whipping cream, heavy
- 1 quartered onion, medium
- 2 eggs, large
- 2 tbsp. of melted butter, unsalted
- 1 tsp. of salt, kosher
- 1/4 tsp. of nutmeg, ground
- Pepper, ground, as desired

Instructions:

Preheat the oven to 390F.

Mix water & flour together in bowl till it forms thin paste. Add additional water if you need to.

Combine the flour mixture with cream, chicken livers, eggs, onions, butter, nutmeg, kosher salt & ground pepper in food processor. Then process for 30-45 seconds, till smooth and blended.

Transfer the liver mixture into 3 x 1" x 4" disposable pans. Use foil to cover them. Place in baking pan. Pour water in pan till it comes halfway up pan sides.

Bake in 390F oven for 20-25 minutes. Then remove the foil. Continue to bake for 20-25 minutes, till cooked through. Temperature in center should be 165F. Allow to cool down to typical room temperature. Serve on bread. Cover leftovers with lids and place in the refrigerator.

16 – Denmark Pork Chops

Denmark is known around the world for its pork, believed to be among the finest you can find. This pork chop recipe is so delicious that guests may think you're an even better cook than you actually are.

Makes 4 Servings

Cooking + Prep Time: 1 & 1/2 hours

Ingredients:

- 4 pork chops, trimmed
- Kosher salt & ground pepper, as desired
- Breadcrumbs – enough to cover chops
- 1 egg, large
- To fry: shortening

Instructions:

Preheat oven to 325F.

Mix kosher salt & ground pepper as desired into breadcrumbs.

Lightly whip the egg.

Turn chops in whipped egg. Coat with breadcrumbs.

Heat the butter in large frying pan.

Lightly brown the porkchops on each side. Place in shallow baking dish.

Pour the drippings over pork chops.

Cover baking dish. Bake in 325F oven for 40-45 minutes, till done through. Serve.

17 – Danish Potato Soup

This is a soulful, smooth soup that is always a big hit when I take it to dinner parties during the winter months. It's true comfort food.

Makes 4 Servings

Cooking + Prep Time: 1 hour

Ingredients:

- 1 tbsp. of butter, unsalted
- 3 peeled, finely diced potatoes, russet
- 1 chopped onion, medium
- 2 cups of veggie broth, low sodium
- 6 tbsp. of cheese, mascarpone
- Salt, kosher & pepper, black, as desired
- 1/2 tsp. of lemon juice, fresh +/- as desired
- 4 x 1-oz. slices of gravlax (smoked salmon, sliced thinly)
- 2 tbsp. of cheese, mascarpone
- 1 tbsp. of chopped chives, fresh

Instructions:

Melt the butter in pan on low heat. Stir while cooking potatoes & onions for three minutes, till onion starts becoming translucent.

Increase the heat up to med. Add veggie broth. Bring to boil. Reduce the heat to low. Cover pan and simmer for 14-15 minutes, till potatoes become tender.

Pour mixture into large sized bowl. Puree and return to pan. Bring soup back to simmer on med-low. Whisk in the 6 tbsp. of cheese. Add lemon juice and season as desired.

Preheat the oven to 200F. Warm four oven-safe bowls for five minutes.

Roll smoked salmon slice loosely into the shape of a rose. Pinch at bottom and fan out top. One salmon rosette goes into bottom of each warmed bowl. Pour soup gently over rosette. Drizzle each soup bowl with 1/2 tbsp. cheese. Use chives for garnishing. Serve.

18 – Denmark Potato Salad

Potatoes are more than just fillers in Danish recipes. Expect them to be prepared into a delightful dish whenever they are used. This potato salad is an authentic recipe from Denmark, and your family and friends will love it.

Makes 4 Servings

Cooking + Prep Time: 45 minutes + 1 hour chilling time

Ingredients:

- 2 lb. of boiled, sliced potatoes
- 2 hard-boiled, chopped eggs, large
- 2 tbsp. of shallot onions, chopped finely
- 3 to 5 celery stalks, chopped finely
- 1 cucumber, chopped finely
- 2 tbsp. of vinegar
- 2 to 3 tsp. of salt, kosher
- 1/2 cup of cream, heavy
- 1/2 tsp. of pepper, black
- 3 tsp. of mustard, French
- 2 to 3 tbsp. of vinegar
- 3 & 1/2 oz. of mayonnaise, reduced fat
- 1 tsp. of lemon juice, fresh

To garnish:

- 1 large egg, hardboiled
- 1 tomato, medium
- Parsley, chopped, fresh

Instructions:

Cut potatoes in cubes. Pour in large bowl.

Add eggs, onions, cucumbers and celery to bowl.

Mix the vinegar with cream, kosher salt & ground pepper and add to bowl.

Allow mixture to set for 10-12 minutes. Add mayo.

Place salad in refrigerator for an hour or so.

Add lemon juice. Season as desired.

If salad seems a bit dry, you can add some more cream.

Add tomatoes, egg & parsley to salad top. Serve.

19 – Danish Ollebrod Beer Soup

This simple, traditional Danish soup is commonly served as a one-dish meal, served with beer to drink. This is one of the most often prepared beer soup recipes. Different local areas have variations of it.

Makes 4 Servings

Cooking + Prep Time: 35 minutes + 3 hours soaking time

Ingredients:

- 8 pumpernickel bread slices, torn in small-sized pieces
- Optional: 1 cup of water, filtered
- 2 cups of ale, dark + extra if desired
- 1 juiced, zested lemon, fresh
- A pinch of sugar, granulated, as desired
- Optional: 1/4 cup of whipping cream, heavy

Instructions:

Place the bread in large pan. Cover with water and ale. Allow to soak for three hours or longer.

Bring the bread and ale mixture to simmer on low heat. Cook for 15-20 minutes, till mixture thickens. Puree with immersion blender till smooth. Stir in the lemon juice and zest & sugar. Bring to boil. Ladle soup in individual bowls. Top with whipping cream and serve.

20 – Amager Stew

This is a Danish farmer's meal that traditionally came from the Island of Amager, locating near Copenhagen. It's a hearty stew that makes for a wonderful meal on cold evenings.

Makes 4 Servings

Cooking + Prep Time: 50 minutes

Ingredients:

- 1 lb. of smoked pork saddle or ham
- 1 lb. of carrots
- 17 fluid oz. of water, filtered
- 1 lb. of potatoes, new
- 1/2 lb. of peas, shelled
- 1 tbsp. of butter, unsalted
- 2 tsp. of flour, all-purpose
- Salt, kosher, as desired
- Pepper, ground, as desired
- 1 bundle of parsley, chopped

Instructions:

Cut pork or ham in small cubes.

Peel carrots and potatoes. Cut in cubes as well.

Shell peas. Discard pods.

Boil pork or ham with carrots and potatoes till almost cooked fully through. Add peas.

Mix flour into butter. Add to mixture. Allow to boil for five more minutes. Season as desired. Top dish with parsley and serve.

21 – Danish Red Cabbage

This side dish is best served beside roast duck or pork, meatballs or pork chops. It's an especially popular dish during the Christmas season.

Makes 6 Servings

Cooking + Prep Time: 1 hour & 25 minutes

Ingredients:

- 2 lb. of cabbage, red
- 2 tbsp. of butter, unsalted
- 1/4 cup of vinegar, white, distilled
- 1 cup of juice, cranberry
- 2 tbsp. of sugar, granulated + extra as desired
- Salt, kosher, as desired

Instructions:

Remove outer cabbage leaves. Discard them. Cut the cabbage in quarters, then remove & discard the white stem. Finely chop the rest of the cabbage.

Melt the butter in pot on med. heat. Stir while cooking cabbage in butter for two to three minutes, till slightly softened. Pour vinegar atop cabbage. Stir, coating well. Add the sugar and cranberry juice. Season mixture as desired.

Reduce the heat level to low. Cover the pot. Stir occasionally while cooking for 60-75 minutes, till cabbage becomes fully tender. Add additional sugar if too tart. Serve.

22 – Potatoes with Onions & Bacon

This filling meal was once mainly popular with poor farm families in Denmark. It's satisfying, inexpensive and easy to make. It's a good way for outsiders of Denmark to try a traditional Danish meal.

Makes 4 Servings

Cooking + Prep Time: 1 hour & 10 minutes

Ingredients:

- 1 lb. of potatoes
- 2 onions, medium
- 2 tsp. of parsley or chives
- Salt, kosher, as desired
- Pepper, black, as desired
- 2 tbsp. of butter, unsalted
- 1/2 lb. of bacon, lean

Instructions:

Peel potatoes & boil in unsalted, filtered water till tender, 20 to 25 minutes. They need to be tender enough that you can mash them.

Cut bacon in small-sized cubes. Fry in pan. Place on paper towels to drain. Reserve grease.

Chop the onions. Fry in bacon grease.

Mash potatoes. Mix with softened butter & kosher salt. Top with bacon and onions. Sprinkle with parsley or chives and serve.

23 – Danish Veal & Pork Meatballs

This recipe comes directly from Denmark. It is served warm with sauce, boiled red potatoes & cabbage.

Makes 6 Servings

Cooking + Prep Time: 1 & 1/4 hours

Ingredients:

- 1/2 lb. of veal, ground
- 1/2 lb. of pork, ground
- 1/4 cup of onion, grated finely
- 1/4 cup of milk, +/- as needed
- 1 egg, large
- 1/4 cup of breadcrumbs + extra if needed
- 1/4 cup of flour, all-purpose
- 1/4 cup of seltzer water
- Kosher salt, as desired
- Ground pepper, as desired
- 1/4 cup of margarine

Instructions:

Mix pork & veal together in medium bowl. Stir in milk, egg and onions. Mix breadcrumbs into meat. Sprinkle in flour. Mix well by kneading.

Stir in seltzer water, then season as desired. Combine well. The mixture needs to be moist, but it shouldn't be dripping.

Chill meat mixture in refrigerator for 15-30 minutes.

Heat margarine in skillet on med. heat.

Scoop 2 & 1/2 tbsp. +/- of meat mixture for each meatball you'll be forming. They should be oval, flattened a bit and roughly the size of small eggs.

Place meatballs in skillet. Fry for 12-15 minutes each side, till no pink remains and meatballs have browned well. Serve.

24 – Pot Roast & Gravy

This delicious Danish dish isn't something you'll serve every day. It is usually served on special occasions and holidays.

Makes 8 Servings

Cooking + Prep Time: 3 hours & 45 minutes

Ingredients:

- 5 lb. of roast, trimmed
- 2 tsp. of salt, kosher
- 1 tsp. of pepper, white
- 3 tbsp. of butter, unsalted
- 1 large onion, sliced
- 1/2 cup of water, filtered
- 3/4 cup of wine, red
- 1 cup of cream
- 2 tbsp. of flour, all-purpose
- 3 garlic cloves

Instructions:

Preheat oven to 320F

Rub roast with kosher salt & white pepper, as desired.

Heat the butter in large frying pan. Brown roast on each side.

Place the roast in roasting pan. Put garlic and sliced onions on top. Add water, wine and cream.

Cook in 320F oven for 3 hours, till roast becomes tender. If bottom of pan gets dry, add more wine.

Remove from oven and place the roast on large platter.

Blend the flour into roasting pan liquid, making gravy. Serve roast with potatoes & gravy.

25 – Danish Dilled Shrimp

Holiday meals in Denmark aren't complete without dilled shrimp. It's popular with guests at all kinds of holiday parties and buffet dinners.

Makes 8 Servings

Cooking + Prep Time: 50 minutes + 8 hours (overnight) chilling time

Ingredients:

- 2 quarts of water, filtered
- 1/4 cup of salt, coarse
- 1/3 cup of sugar, granulated
- 5 dill sprigs
- 2 lb. of shrimp, medium, shells included
- 2 tbsp. of oil, vegetable
- 1 tbsp. of vinegar, white wine
- 1 tbsp. of dill, minced
- 1/4 tsp. of salt, kosher
- 1/4 tsp. of pepper, black

Instructions:

Bring the water to boil in large-sized pot on high heat. Then add the coarse salt, granulated sugar & sprigs of dill. Stir till sugar dissolves.

Add shrimp to pot. Cook for three to four minutes, till shells have turned pink and shrimp aren't translucent anymore. Strain shrimp through colander and discard the dill. Chill for 1/2 hour or so in refrigerator, till cold.

After shrimp cool, peel & devein them and discard their shells.

Whisk vinegar, oil, minced dill, kosher salt & black pepper. Toss with shrimp, coating well. Cover the dish. Place in refrigerator and allow to chill overnight. Serve with fresh dill sprigs.

Delicious Dessert Recipes from Denmark...

26 – Denmark Apple Dessert

This is called a cake, but it's actually not a cake in the traditional sense. It's made up of layers that consist of stewed apples, then caramelized oats and whipped cream.

Makes 6-8 Servings

Cooking + Prep Time: 50 minutes

Ingredients:

- 1 lb. of apples, tart
- 1 lb. of apples, sweet
- 3 tbsp. of sugar, granulated
- 2 tsp. of sugar, vanilla
- 1 & 3/4 oz. of butter, unsalted
- 7 oz. of oats, rolled
- 4 & 1/2 oz. of sugar, granulated
- 1 & 1/4 cups of cream, whipping
- 1 tbsp. of plain chocolate, grated

Instructions:

Fill large pot with filtered water.

Peel the apples, then core them and slice them finely. Drop into the water.

Drain the water except for 1 tbsp. Cover pot. Stew apples along with 3 tbsp. of granulated sugar & the vanilla sugar for 10-14 minutes, till apples are tender.

Transfer stewed apples to bowl. Let them cool.

In large pan, melt butter on low heat. Add sugar and stir.

Once sugar caramelizes with the butter, which typically takes 2-3 minutes, stir in oats till toasted and golden, being sure not to burn them. Allow them to cool.

Whip the cream. Place 1/2 of apple mixture in large bowl. Follow with 1/2 toasted oats. Repeat the layers. Top with single layer of whipped cream. Sprinkle with the grated chocolate and serve.

27 – Light Cherry Danish Dessert

This is an easy, light recipe for a dessert made with Danish pastry. You can use jam instead of pie filling if you like.

Makes 24 Servings

Cooking + Prep Time: 1 hour & 10 minutes

Ingredients:

- 2 x 8-oz. cans of dinner rolls, crescent, refrigerated
- 2 x 8-oz. pkgs. of cream cheese, reduced fat
- 1 & 1/2 cups of sugar, powdered
- 1 egg white, large
- 1 tsp. of vanilla extract, pure
- 1 x 21-oz. can of pie filling, cherry
- 1 tbsp. of milk, skim, +/- as necessary

Instructions:

Preheat the oven to 350F. Grease 13" x 9" casserole dish.

Place contents from one can of dinner rolls into greased dish. Press into bottom of dish, forming a crust. Seal together by pressing the seams firmly.

Beat the cream cheese with 3/4 cup of powdered sugar, vanilla extract and egg white with hand mixer at med. speed till blended well. Spread onto the crust.

Spread the pie filling over cream cheese mixture.

Put second roll of dough onto wax paper sheet and form a rectangle the same size as your casserole dish. Press the seams together and seal. Invert this dough over the pie filling, forming the top crust. Discard the wax paper.

Bake in 350F oven for 30-35 minutes, till golden brown. Allow to cool for 20 minutes or longer.

Stream the milk into last 3/4 cup of powdered sugar in medium bowl while beating, till thick and blended well. Drizzle over the dessert. Slice in 24 pieces and serve.

28 – Denmark Dessert Aebleskiver "Pancake Balls"

This is a spherical, warm, and puffy pancake ball that is usually eaten at night. The powdered sugar and strawberry jam make it a wonderful dessert.

Makes 12 Servings

Cooking + Prep Time: 30 minutes

Ingredients:

- 2 egg whites, large
- 2 egg yolks, large
- 2 cups of flour, all-purpose
- 1/2 tsp. of baking soda
- 2 tsp. of baking powder
- 4 tbsp. of melted butter, unsalted
- 1 tbsp. of sugar, granulated
- 1/2 tsp. of salt, kosher
- 2 cups of buttermilk, low fat
- For decorating/filling: strawberry jam (or your favorite jam)
- For sprinkling: powdered sugar
- To grease pan: additional butter, melted

Instructions:

In medium bowl, beat egg whites till they hold stiff peaks. Set them aside.

Mix together flour, baking soda, baking powder, egg yolks, sugar, buttermilk and the 4 tbsp. of melted butter. Beat till smooth. Fold in egg whites.

Brush bottoms of Aebleskiver pan cups using melted butter. Heat till they are hot.

Pour in 2 tbsp. batter per cup. When their edges are bubbling, flip over with fork. Continue to cook till balls are cooked through like pancakes and golden brown in color.

Serve with syrup or jam. Use powdered sugar to sprinkle.

29 – Danish Sponge Cake

This moist and airy sponge cake topped with caramelized coconut may become a favorite in your house, as it is in ours. It's tasty from your first bite to your last!

Makes 10-12 Servings

Cooking + Prep Time: 1 hour & 10 minutes

Ingredients:

- 3 eggs, whole
- 1 cup of sugar, granulated
- 1 tsp. of vanilla extract, pure
- 1 & 3/4 cups of flour, all-purpose
- 6 tbsp. of milk, whole
- 6 tbsp. of melted butter, unsalted
- 2 tsp. of baking powder

For the Topping

- 1 stick of butter, unsalted
- 1 & 1/2 cups of unsweetened coconut, shredded
- 1 cup of sugar, dark brown
- 3 tbsp. of milk, whole

Instructions:

Preheat oven to 375F. Butter & flour 9" springform pan that is 3" deep.

In small pan, combine the milk with 6 tbsp. of butter. Heat on low till butter has melted. Remove from heat. Allow butter to cool a bit.

Next, use a hand mixer and large bowl to whisk the eggs, vanilla and sugar for 4-5 minutes at high speed. Mixture should be fluffy and white. Add baking powder and flour and incorporate them into the mixture by whisking.

Pour the milk & butter mixture into cake batter and fold till incorporated well. Pour batter in prepared pan. Then, place on cookie sheet lined with parchment paper.

Bake in 375F oven for 35 to 40 minutes, till nearly done.

To prepare topping, melt the butter in med. pan. Add milk & brown sugar. Cook for one minute. Add coconut shreds. Mix well.

Then, remove cake from oven. Spread carefully with topping.

Turn oven heat up to 400F. Return cake to oven. Bake for 5-10 more minutes till topping becomes bubbly and coconut starts toasting.

Remove cake from the oven. Let it cool and serve.

30 – Denmark Spice Cookies

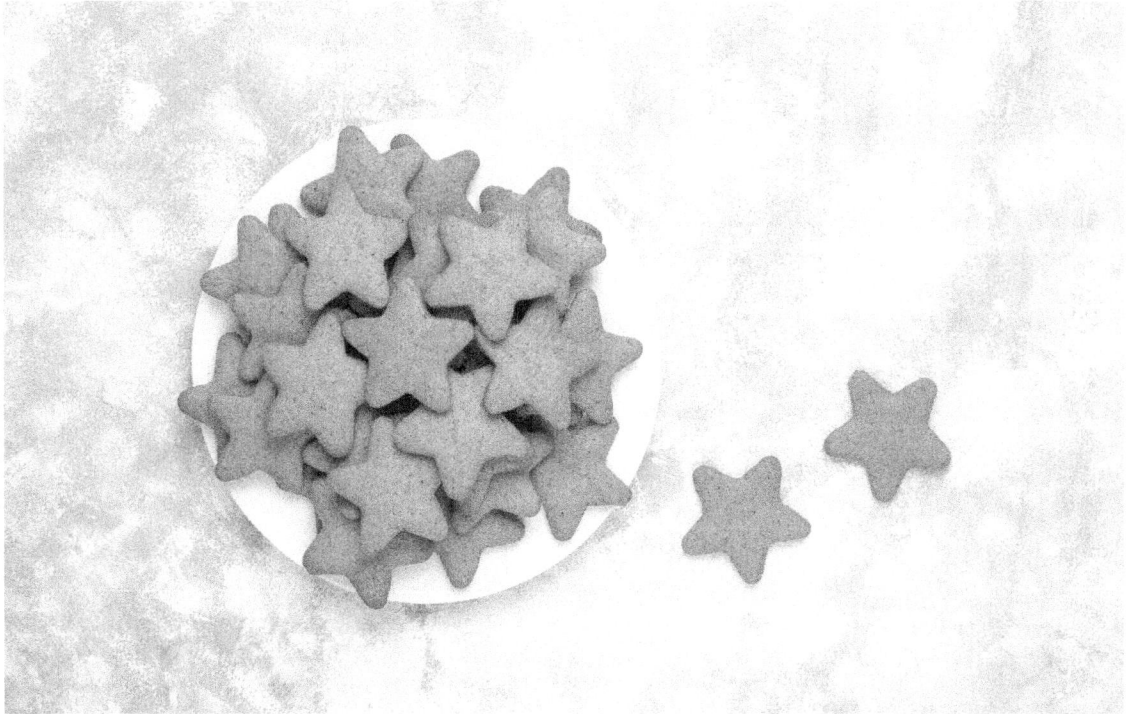

These are little, tasty spiced cookies. They seem plain at first sight, but they are actually quite addictive. They're a bit like vanilla wafers with more flavor.

Makes 100 cookies +/-

Cooking + Prep Time: 30 minutes

Ingredients:

- 1 cup of butter, unsalted
- 1 cup of sugar, granulated
- 2 eggs, large
- 2 & 1/2 cups of flour, all-purpose
- 1 tsp. of cardamom, ground
- 1 tsp. of cinnamon, ground +/- as desired

Instructions:

Preheat oven to 350F.

In large-sized bowl, mix butter & sugar together till the mixture is smooth. Beat the eggs in one after another and stir till fluffy and light.

Combine flour, cinnamon and cardamom. Stir this into sugar and butter mixture till barely blended.

Separate dough in six balls. Roll them into ropes on floured work surface. They should be roughly the circumference of your finger. Cut in 1/2" pieces. Place on non-greased cookie sheet.

Bake dough in 350F oven till lightly browned, 8-10 minutes. Cool on cookie sheets for several minutes. Transfer to wire racks and allow to completely cool. Serve.

Conclusion

This Denmark cookbook has shown you…

How to use different ingredients to affect unique, welcome tastes in many Danish dishes.

How can you include Denmark recipes in your home repertoire?

You can…

Make breakfast buns and Danish pancakes with bacon & eggs, which you may have heard of before. They are just as mouthwatering tasty as they sound.

Cook soups and stews, which are widely served in Denmark homes. Find ingredients in meat & produce or frozen food sections of your local grocery stores.

Enjoy making delectable Danish seafood dishes, including shrimp and cod. Fish is a mainstay in the recipes year-round, and there are SO many ways to make it great.

Make dishes using potatoes and pasta in recipes from Denmark. Potatoes are a staple there, and they use them in many creative ways.

Make all kinds of desserts like Danish spice cookies and sponge cake, which will surely tempt anyone with a sweet tooth.

Enjoy the recipes with your family and friends!

About the Author

Allie Allen developed her passion for the culinary arts at the tender age of five when she would help her mother cook for their large family of 8. Even back then, her family knew this would be more than a hobby for the young Allie and when she graduated from high school, she applied to cooking school in London. It had always been a dream of the young chef to study with some of Europe's best and she made it happen by attending the Chef Academy of London.

After graduation, Allie decided to bring her skills back to North America and open up her own restaurant. After 10 successful years as head chef and owner, she decided to sell her business and pursue other career avenues. This monumental decision led Allie to her true calling, teaching. She also started to write e-books for her students to study at home for practice. She is now the proud author of several e-books and gives private and semi-private cooking lessons to a range of students at all levels of experience.

Stay tuned for more from this dynamic chef and teacher when she releases more informative e-books on cooking and baking in the near future. Her work is infused with stores and anecdotes you will love!

Author's Afterthoughts

I can't tell you how grateful I am that you decided to read my book. My most heartfelt thanks that you took time out of your life to choose my work and I hope you find benefit within these pages.

There are so many books available today that offer similar content so that makes it even more humbling that you decided to buying mine.

Tell me what you thought! I am eager to hear your opinion and ideas on what you read as are others who are looking for a good book to buy. Leave a review on Amazon.com so others can benefit from your wisdom!

With much thanks,

Allie Allen

Printed in Great Britain
by Amazon

35604197R00051